HAL LEONARD STUDENT PIANO LIBRARY

Level 5

God Bless America®
and Other Patriotic Piano Duets
For One Piano, Four Hands

Complements All Piano Methods

Table of Contents

God Bless America And Other Patriotic Piano Duets Level 5 is designed for use with the fifth book of any piano method.

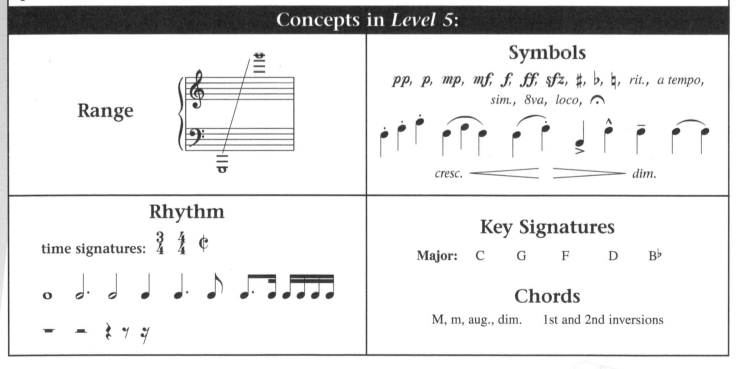

Concepts in *Level 5*:

Range

Symbols

pp, p, mp, mf, f, ff, sfz, ♯, ♭, ♮, *rit., a tempo, sim., 8va, loco,* 𝄐

cresc. ——————— *dim.*

Rhythm

time signatures: ¾ ⁴⁄₄ ¢

Key Signatures

Major: C   G   F   D   B♭

Chords

M, m, aug., dim.   1st and 2nd inversions

ISBN 978-0-634-04081-8

HAL•LEONARD®
CORPORATION
7777 W. BLUEMOUND RD. P.O. BOX 13819 MILWAUKEE, WI 53213

Visit Hal Leonard Online at
www.halleonard.com

God Bless America

Secondo

Words and Music by Irving Berlin
Arranged by Phillip Keveren

With majesty (♩ = 92)

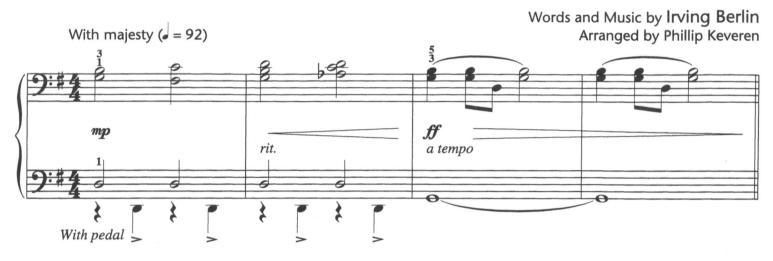

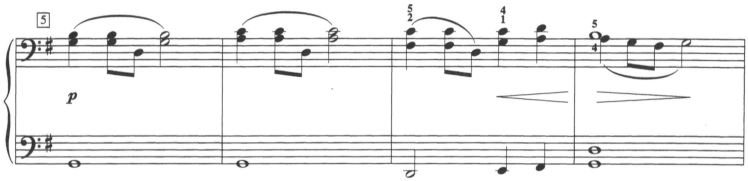

God Bless America

Primo

Words and Music by Irving Berlin
Arranged by Phillip Keveren

With majesty (♩ = 92)

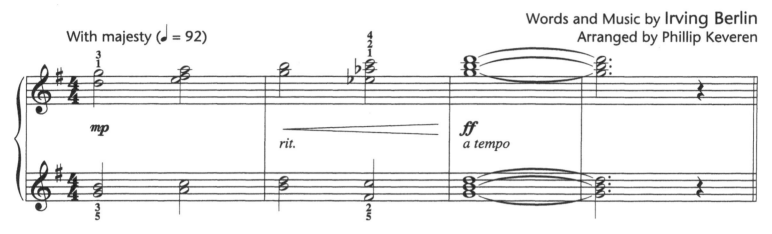

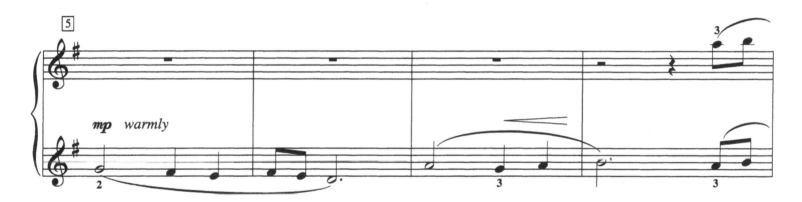

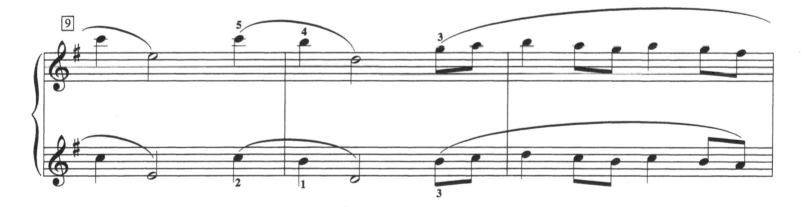

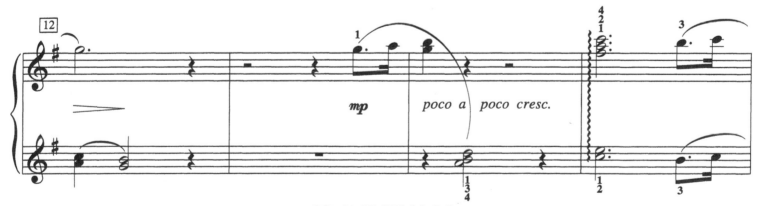

Secondo

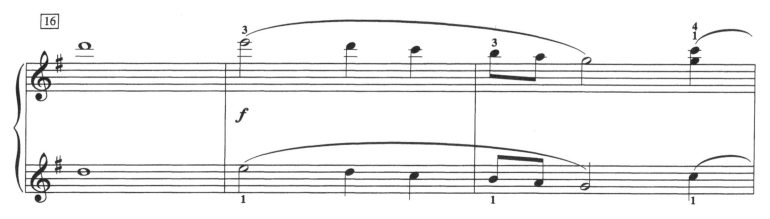

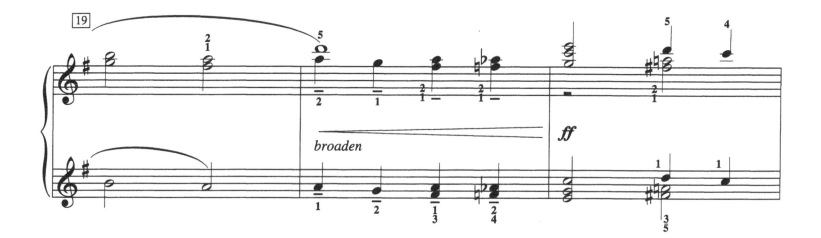

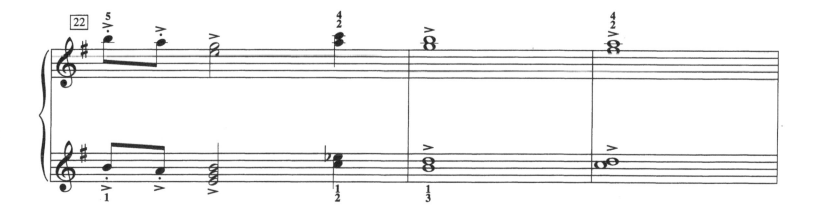

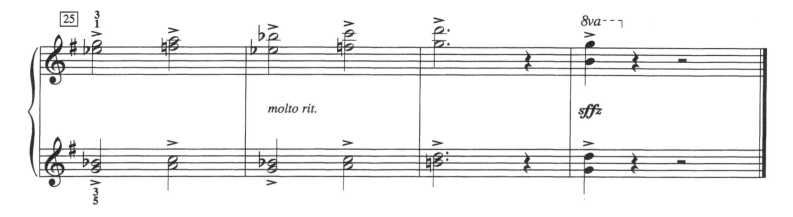

America, The Beautiful

Secondo

Words by Katherine Lee Bates
Music by Samuel A. Ward
Arranged by Christos Tsitsaros

Moderately, with feeling (♩ = 80)

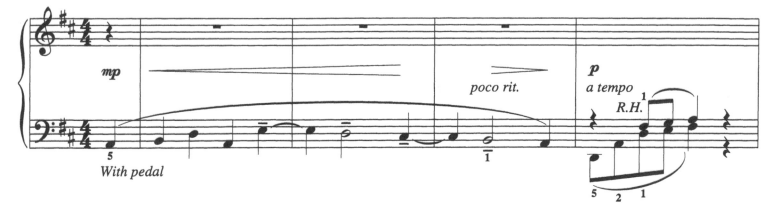

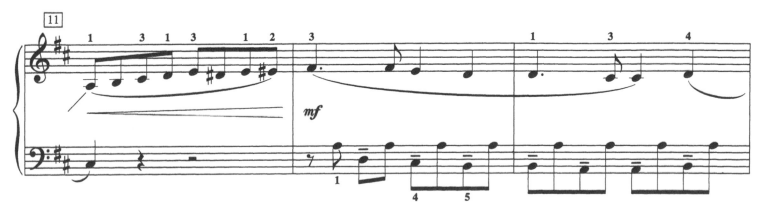

America, The Beautiful

Primo

Words by Katherine Lee Bates
Music by Samuel A. Ward
Arranged by Christos Tsitsaros

Moderately, with feeling (♩ = 80)

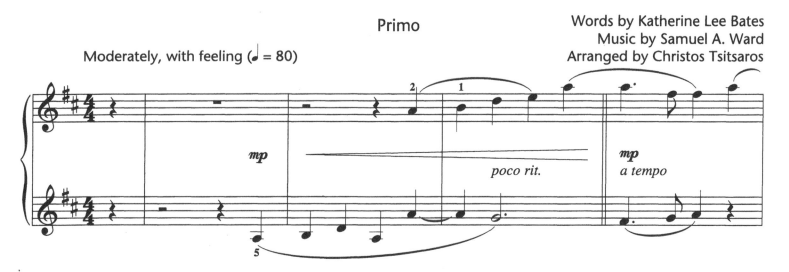

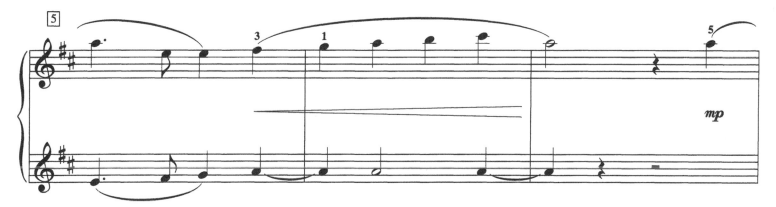

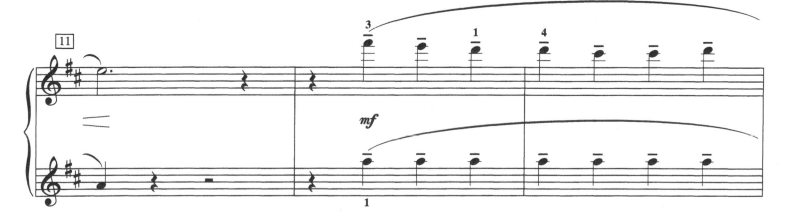

Primo

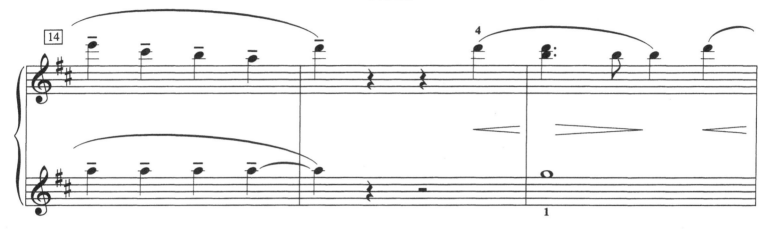

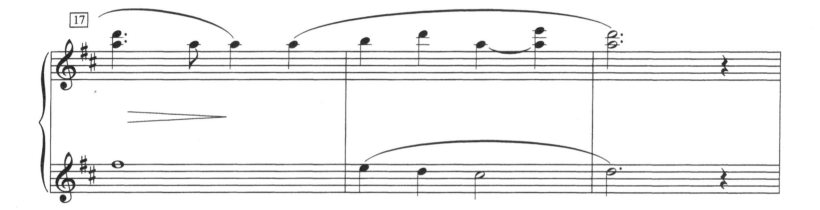

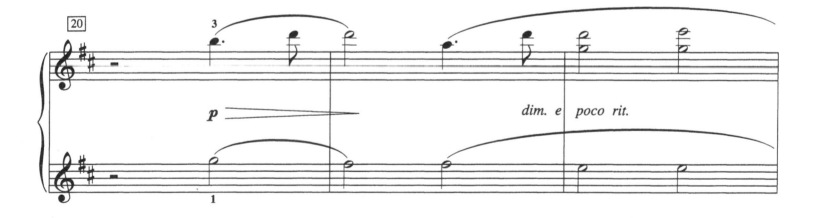

Battle Hymn Of The Republic

Secondo

Words by Julia Ward Howe
Music by William Steffe
Arranged by Fred Kern

Stately March (♩ = 92)

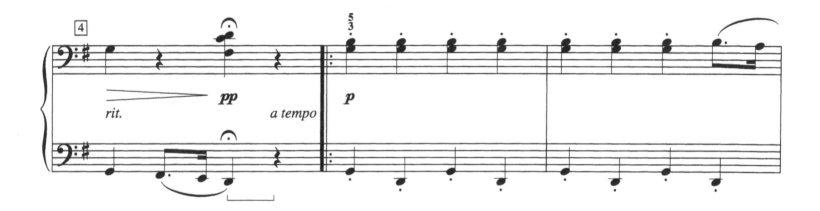

Battle Hymn Of The Republic

For Charles D. Seybold, my duet partner for more than forty years.

Primo

Words by Julia Ward Howe
Music by William Steffe
Arranged by Fred Kern

Stately March (♩ = 92)

Secondo

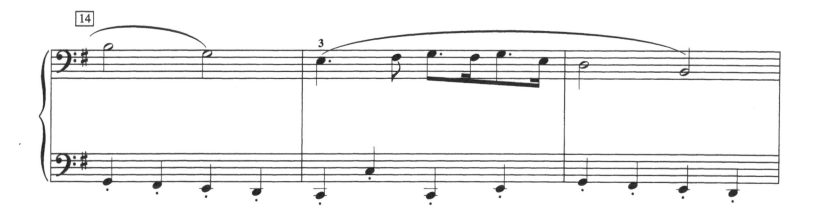

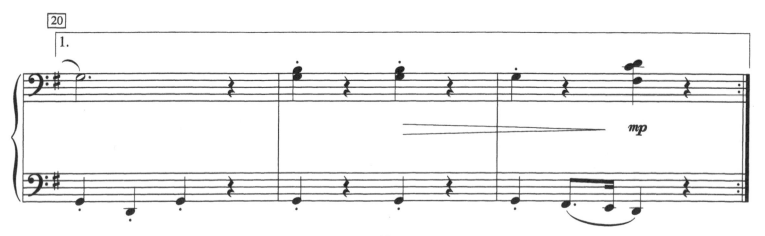

12

Primo

Secondo

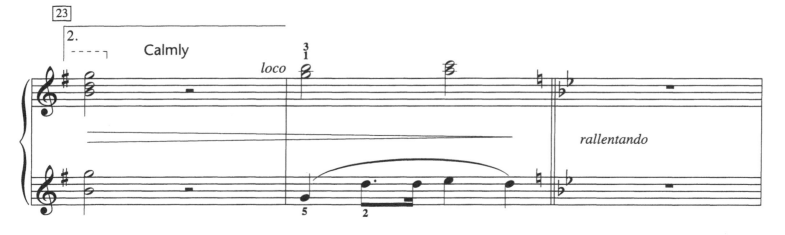

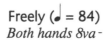

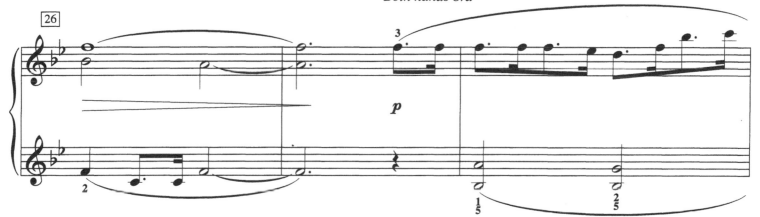

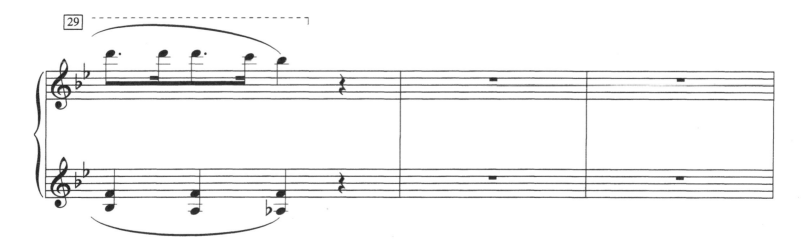

Secondo

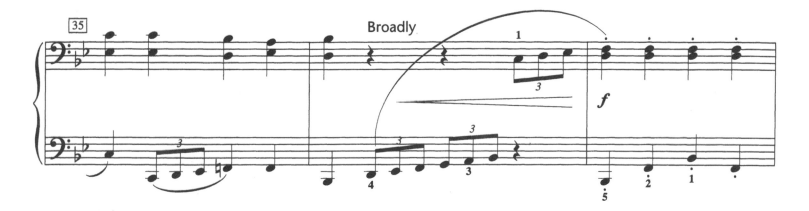

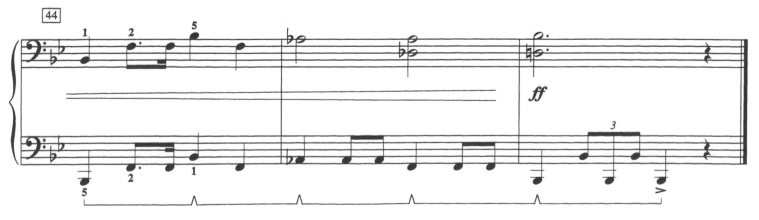

16

Primo

Broadly

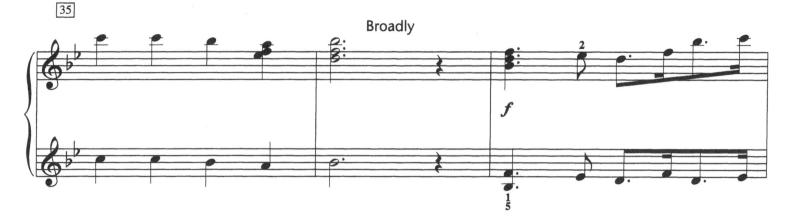

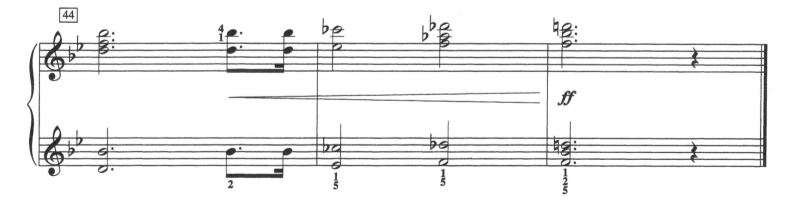

Stars And Stripes Forever

Secondo

By John Philip Sousa
Arranged by Carol Klose

With spirit (♩ = 100)

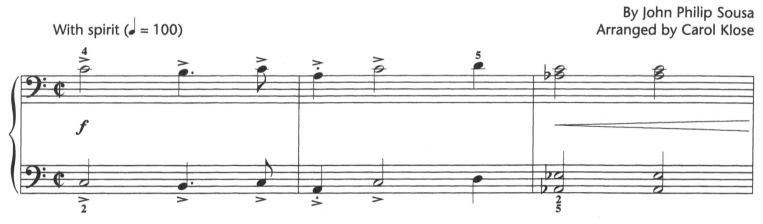

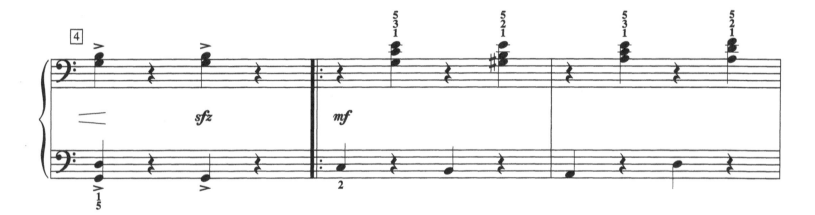

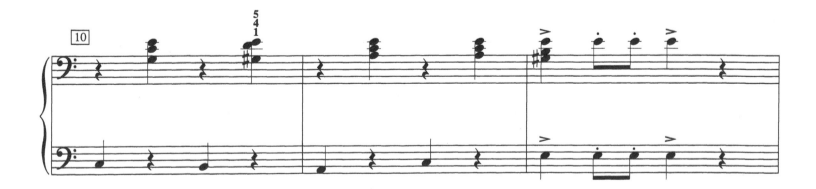

Stars And Stripes Forever

Primo

By John Philip Sousa
Arranged by Carol Klose

With spirit ($\mathbf{\frac{1}{2}}$ = 100)

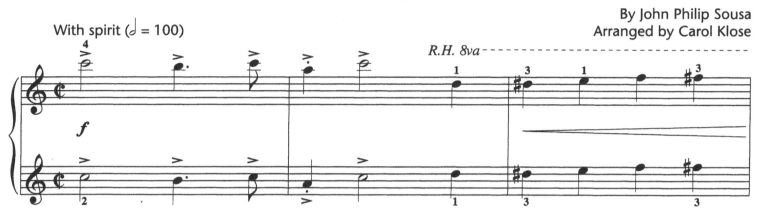

Secondo

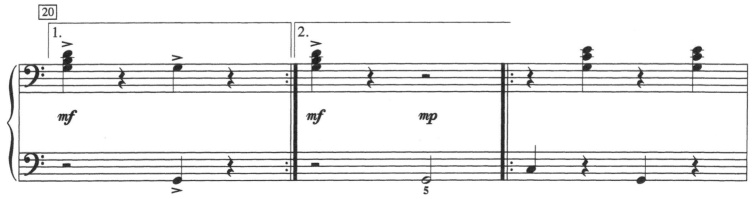

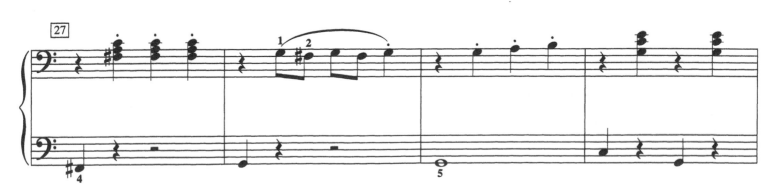

20

Primo

21

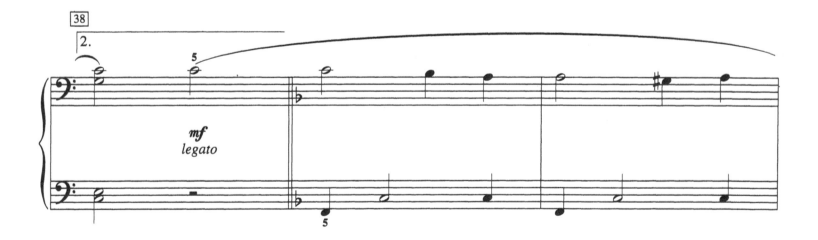

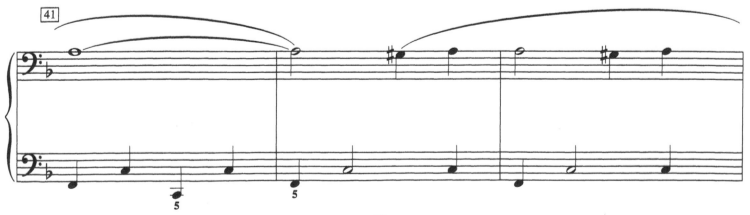

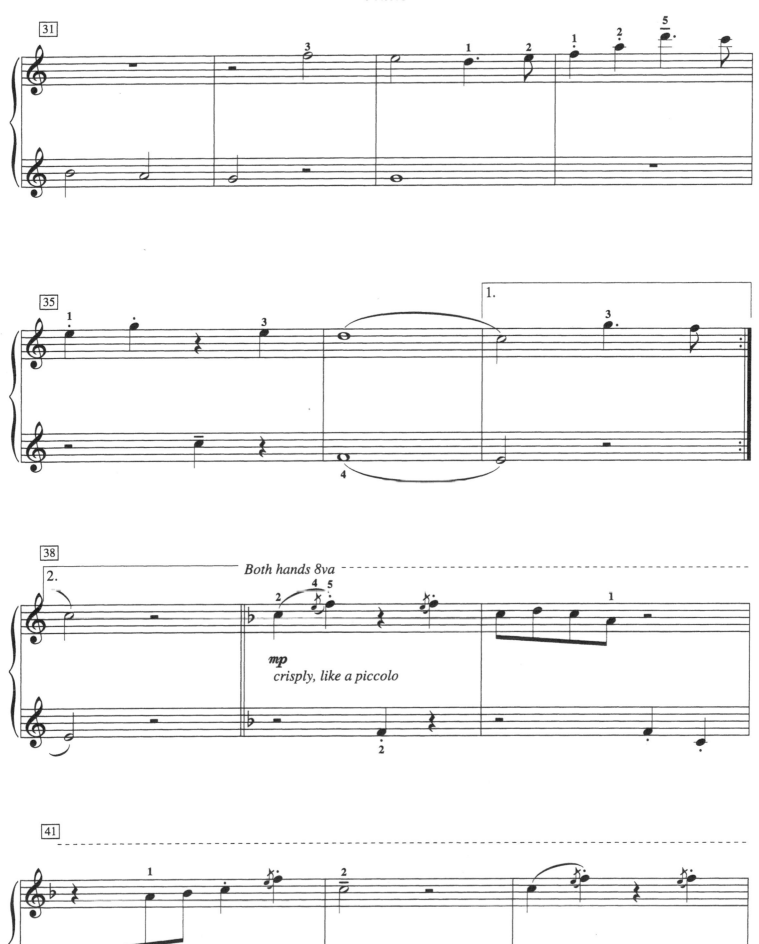

Secondo

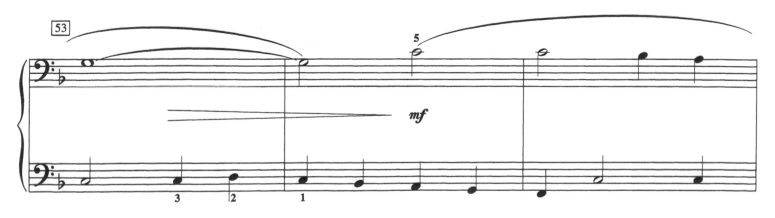

Primo

25

Secondo

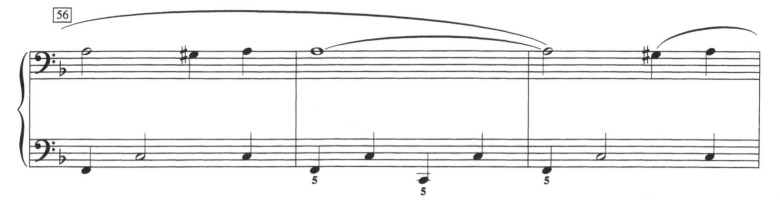

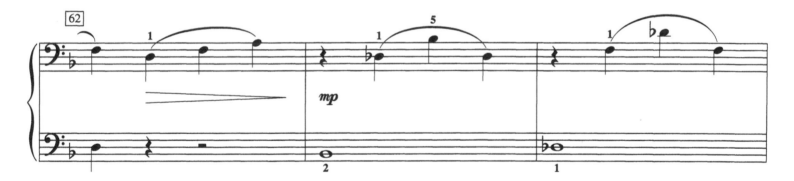

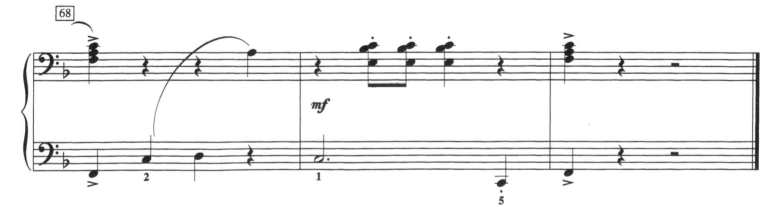

26

Primo

27

The Star Spangled Banner

Secondo

Words by Francis Scott Key
Music by John Stafford Smith
Arranged by Rosemary Barrett Byers

Proudly (♩ = 88-92)

With pedal

The Star Spangled Banner

Primo

Words by Francis Scott Key
Music by John Stafford Smith
Arranged by Rosemary Barrett Byers

Proudly (♩ = 88-92)

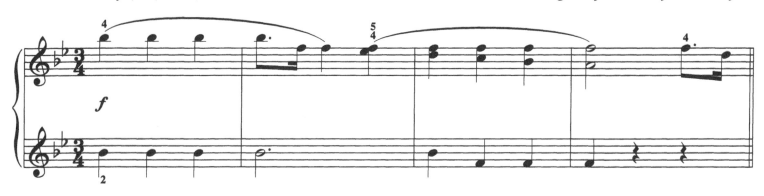

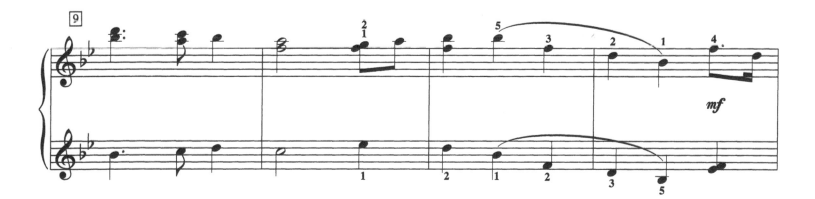

Secondo

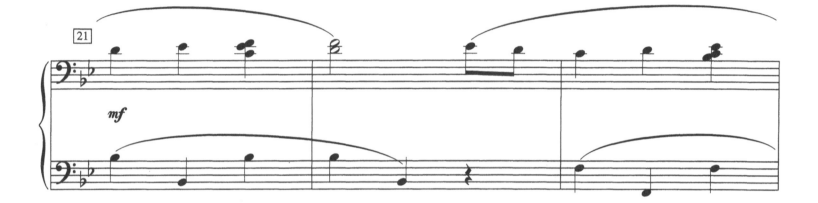

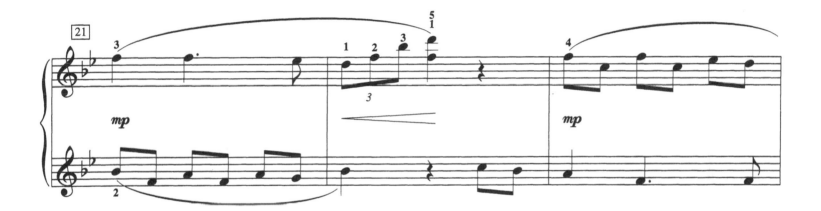

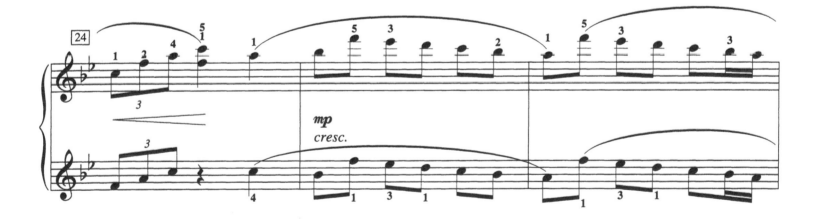

Secondo

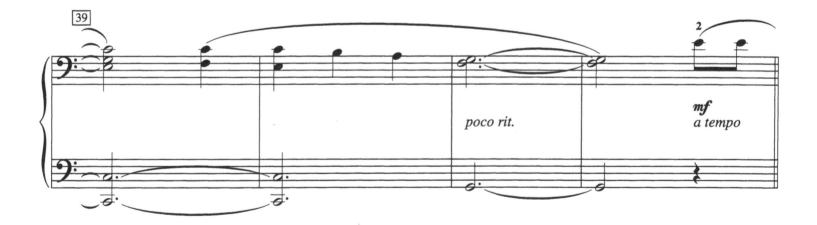

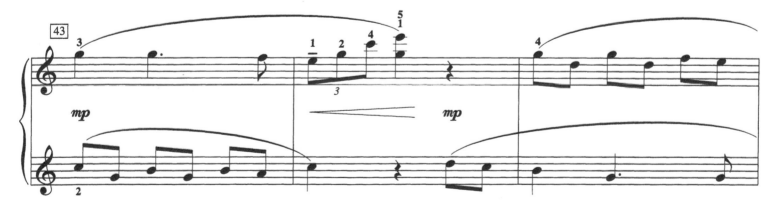

Secondo

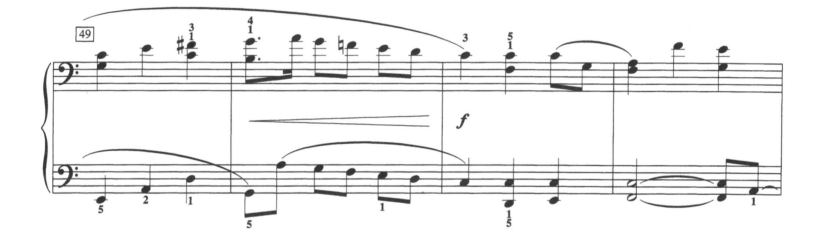

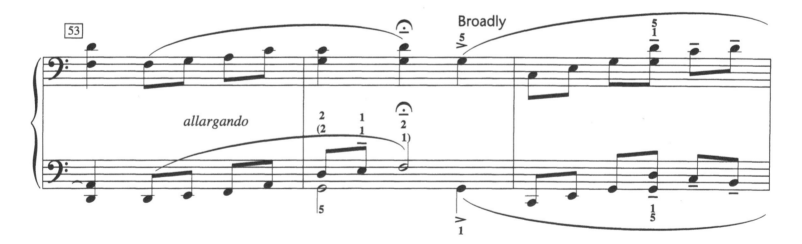

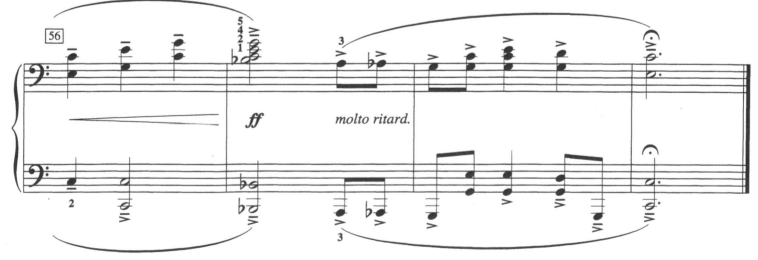

Primo

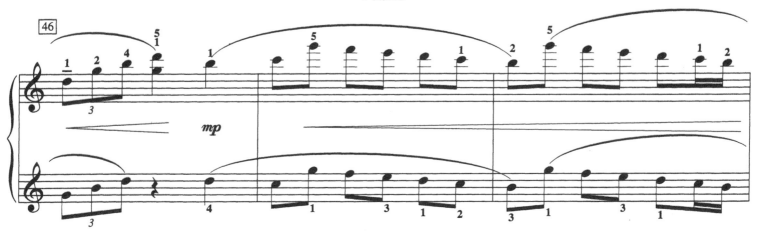

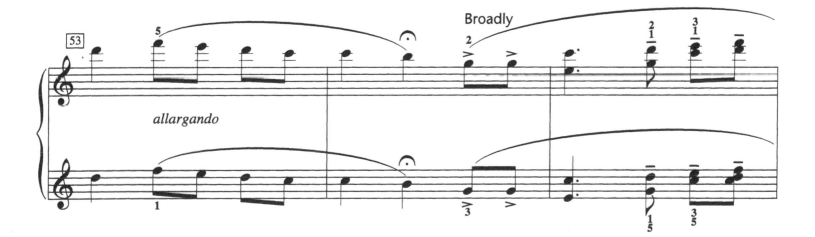

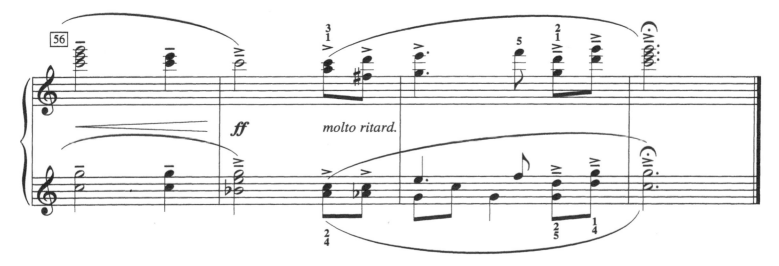

You're A Grand Old Flag

from GEORGE M!

Secondo

Words and Music by George M. Cohan
Arranged by Matthew Edwards

With spirit (♩ = 116)

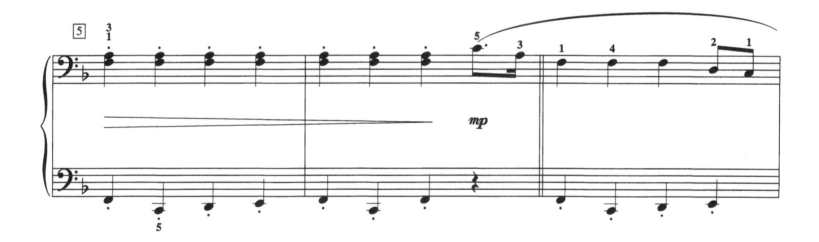

You're A Grand Old Flag

from GEORGE M!

Primo

Words and Music by George M. Cohan
Arranged by Matthew Edwards

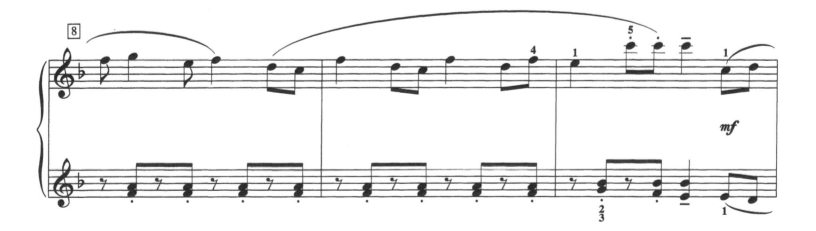

Secondo

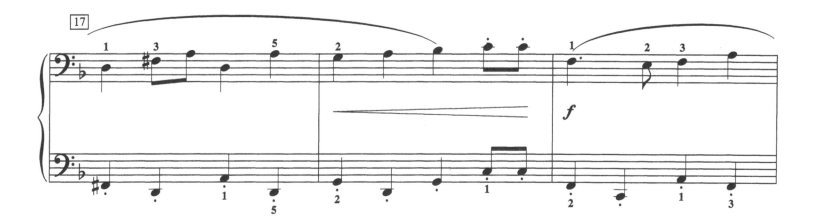

Primo

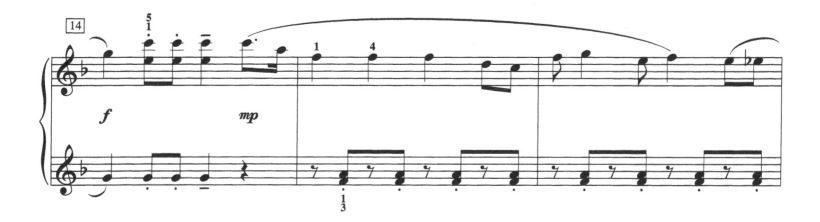

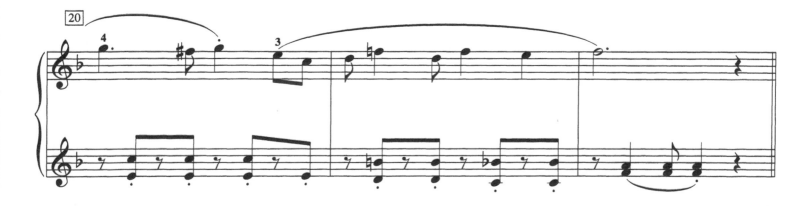

Secondo

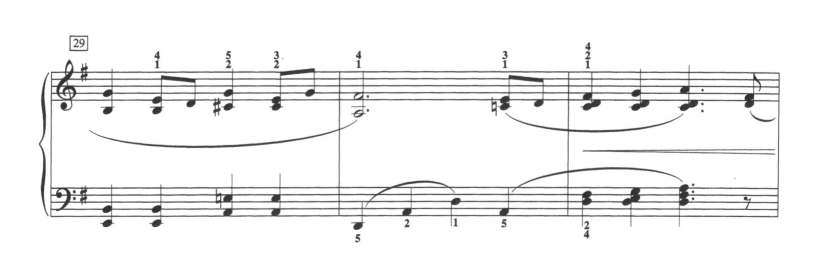

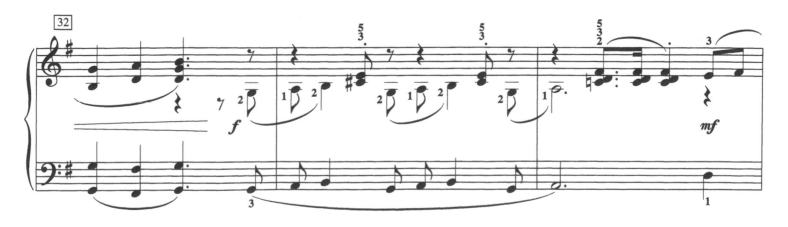

Primo

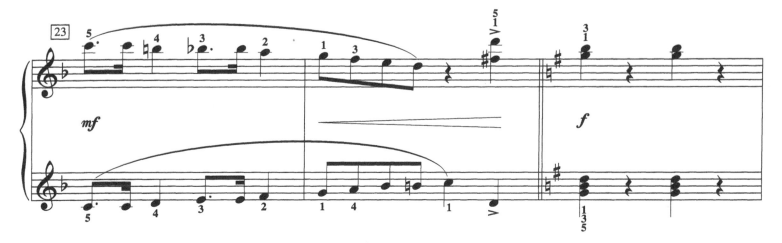

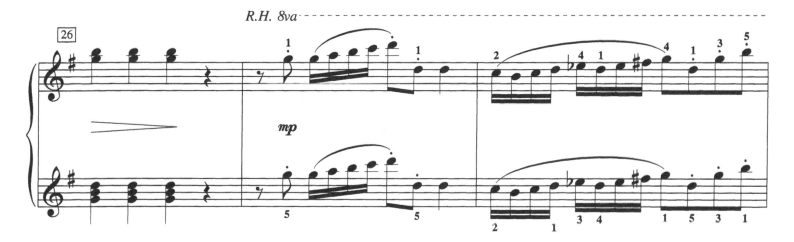

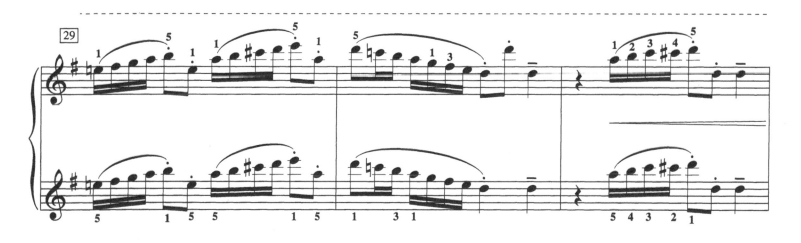

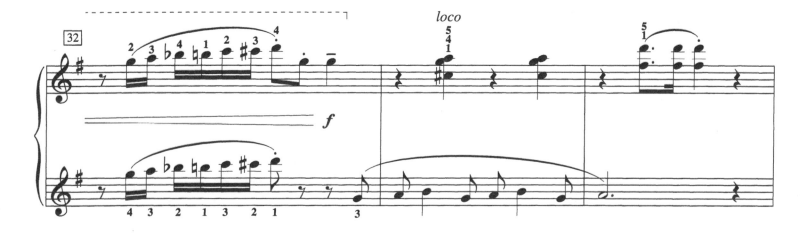

Secondo

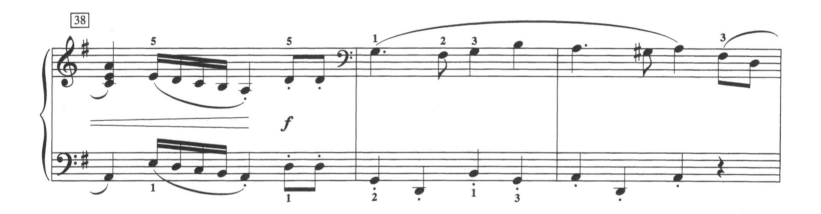

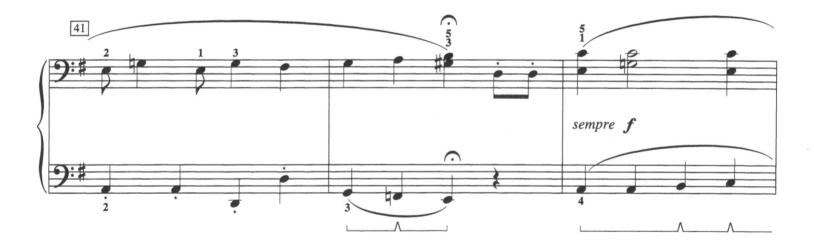

Primo

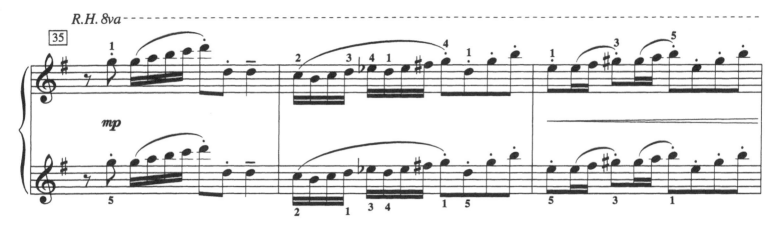

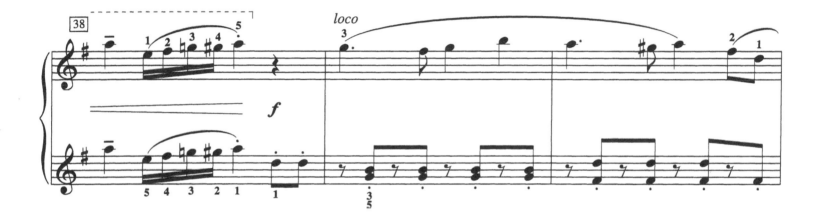

Song Histories And Lyrics

God Bless America
Words and Music by Irving Berlin

This simple, eloquent song captures the hearts of all who hear it. Irving Berlin, who wrote the music and lyrics, is the foremost American song composer of the 20th century. Berlin wrote *God Bless America* in 1918, but the song didn't become known to the public until 1939, when singer Kate Smith performed it on the radio in honor of Armistice Day (Veterans Day). It was an instant hit. Berlin donated his earnings from this song to the Boy and Girl Scouts of America. Over his long lifetime – he lived to celebrate his 101st birthday – Irving Berlin wrote more than 1200 songs, many musicals, and movie scores. His songs are quintessentially American, calling to mind the grand days of Broadway, the Big Band era, and the glamorous Hollywood movies of the 1940s. He is the composer of many classic popular American songs, including: *There's No Business Like Show Business; This Is The Army, Mr. Jones; Alexander's Ragtime Band,* and perhaps his most famous song, *White Christmas,* for which he won an Academy Award. Fellow composer Jerome Kern said of Berlin, "Irving Berlin has no place *in* American music – he *is* American music."

> While the storm clouds gather far across the sea,
> Let us swear allegiance to a land that's free.
> Let us all be grateful for a land so fair,
> As we raise our voices in a solemn prayer.
>
> God bless America, land that I love.
> Stand beside her and guide her
> Thru the night with a light from above.
> From the mountains, to the prairies,
> To the oceans white with foam.
> God bless America, my home sweet home.
> God bless America, my home sweet home.

America, The Beautiful
Words by Katherine Lee Bates
Music by Samuel Ward

Without a doubt, this evocative hymn is the best-known and most-beloved song about America. In fact, there have been many petitions to make this song our national anthem, replacing *The Star-Spangled Banner*. The words were written by a young woman from the East, born in Falmouth, Massachusetts, and educated at Wellesley College, Katherine Lee Bates. She was a woman of uncommon talent, a brilliant poet who dedicated her life to educating women and furthering social causes in support of women's rights and the poor. Her lovely poem to America was inspired, it is said, by a trip to Colorado in 1893, where, with friends, she climbed up Pike's Peak and was inspired by the vast grandeur of the view she saw from the top of the mountain. Her poem was published on July 4, 1895, and eventually was set to music that had been written earlier by Samuel Augustus Ward. Although the words and music were not composed for each other, this song is a superb marriage of words and music, a moving tribute to the beauty that is America.

> O beautiful for spacious skies, for amber waves of grain,
> For purple mountain majesties above the fruited plain!
> America! America! God shed His grace on thee,
> And crown thy good with brotherhood, from sea to shining sea.
>
> O beautiful for pilgrim feet, whose stern, impassioned stress,
> A thoroughfare for freedom beat across the wilderness!
> America! America! God mend thine every flaw,
> Confirm thy soul in self-control, thy liberty in law.
>
> O beautiful for heroes proved in liberating strife,
> Who more than self their country loved and mercy more than life!
> America! America! May God thy gold refine,
> 'Til all success be nobleness and every gain divine.
>
> O beautiful for patriot dream that sees beyond the years.
> Thine alabaster cities gleam, undimmed by human tears!
> America, America! God shed His grace on thee,
> And crown thy good with brotherhood, from sea to shining sea.

Battle Hymn Of The Republic
Words by Katherine Lee Bates
Music by Samuel Ward

This stirring ballad was inspired by Julia Ward Howe's visit to a Union Army camp at the start of the American Civil War in 1861. During a tour of the camp with her husband, a military physician, she heard soldiers singing a popular, but gruesome song, *John Brown's Body Lies A'mould'ring In The Grave.* This song told the story of the radical abolitionist John Brown, who led a brief, violent, and unsuccessful rebellion to free slaves, and who was subsequently hanged for the act. The song was embraced by the North as a tribute to John Brown's raid, and by the South as a sarcastic commentary on his death. Howe sought to counter the opposing purposes of each side, claiming the music for the North with her new, noble lyrics. Her version became the best-known battle hymn of the Union Army. Howe, a talented poet and abolitionist, worked actively for peace and for the rights of women after the American Civil War. She died in 1910, a renowned figure and beloved American matriarch, at the age of ninety-one.

> Mine eyes have seen the glory of the coming of the Lord.
> He is trampling out the vintage where the grapes of wrath are stored.
> He hath loos'd the fateful lightning of His terrible swift sword.
> His truth is marching on. Glory, glory, Hallelujah!
> His truth is marching on.
>
> I have seen him in the watch fires of the hundred circling camps.
> They have builded Him an altar in the evening dews and damps.
> I have read His righteous sentence by the dim and flaring lamps.
> His day is marching on. Glory, glory Hallelujah!
> His day is marching on.
>
> I have read a fiery gospel writ in burnished rows of steel.
> As ye deal with My contemptors, so with you My grace shall deal.
> Let the Hero born of woman crush the serpent with His heel,
> Since God is marching on. Glory, glory Hallelujah!
> Since God is marching on.

He has sounded forth the trumpet that shall never call retreat
He is sifting out the hearts of men before His judgement seat.
O be swift, my soul, to answer Him, be jubilant, my feet,
Our God is marching on. Glory, glory Hallelujah!
Our God is marching on.

In the beauty of the lilies, Christ was born across the sea.
With a glory in His bosom that transfigures you and me.
As He died to make men holy, let us die to make men free,
While God is marching on. Glory, glory Hallelujah!
While God is marching on.

He is coming like the glory of the morning on the wave,
He is wisdom to the mighty, He is honor to the brave.
So the world shall be His footstool, and the soul of wrong His slave,
Our God is marching on. Glory, glory, Hallelujah!
Our God is marching on.

Stars And Stripes Forever
Music by John Philip Sousa

This well-known march was written by John Philip Sousa in 1897, and is often called the Official March of the United States of America. Sousa was born in 1854 in Washington, D.C. and at the young age of 13 he was apprenticed to the Marine Band, the official band of the president of the U.S. He became leader of the Marine Band in 1880 and then resigned that post to form his own band, *Sousa's Band*, in 1892. Sousa and his band made many tours across the U.S. and in Europe, to great acclaim. Known as 'The March King' because of his prolific compositions in this genre, his compositions epitomize an American march – patriotic and rousing in character. His best known marches include the Marine Corps Anthem *Sempre Fidelis*, the *Washington Post March*, and undoubtedly the most popular, *Stars And Stripes Forever*. Sousa also wrote operettas, songs, orchestral compositions, and his autobiography, *Marching Along*. He died in 1932, revered as an original American composer.

The Star Spangled Banner
Words by Francis Scott Key
Music by John Stafford Smith

This song is the national anthem of the United States of America. An American lawyer, Francis Scott Key, wrote the lyrics after he had witnessed the fierce bombardment of Fort McHenry in Baltimore's harbor during the War of 1812. Key had been asked to negotiate the release of an American who had been taken captive by the British. To do so, Key and another negotiator boarded a British warship in Baltimore's harbor where the man was being held. Although the negotiations were successful, the British fleet commander detained Key and the others so that they could not warn the U.S. of the impending attack on the fort. The British fleet's bombardment began on September 13, 1814 and continued all day and night. Key and his colleagues watched the entire night and, in the morning's light, saw the American flag still flying from the walls of the fort. Inspired by this symbol of American freedom, Key pulled an envelope from his pocket and began to write a poem to commemorate the event.

His poem was printed on handbills shortly after the attack on Fort McHenry, with the suggestion to sing the verses to the tune of *To Anacreon In Heaven,* a well-known tune at the time. The song was published as *The Star Spangled Banner* in 1814, and by 1900 it had essentially become the unofficial anthem of the United States. The U.S. Congress passed an act making this song our official national anthem in 1931.

O say, can you see, by the dawn's early light,
What so proudly we hail'd at the twilight's last gleaming?
Whose broad stripes and bright stars, thro' the perilous fight,
O'er the ramparts we watch'd, were so gallantly streaming?
And the rocket's red glare, the bombs bursting in air
Gave proof thro' the night that our flag was still there.
O say, does that star-spangled banner yet wave
O'er the land of the free and the home of the brave?

On the shore dimly seen thro' the mists of the deep,
Where the foe's haughty host in dread silence reposes.
What is that which the breeze, o'er the towering steep,
As it fitfully blows, half conceals, half discloses?
Now it catches the gleam of the morning's first beam,
I full glory reflected now shines in the stream.
'Tis the star-spangled banner oh long may it wave
O'er the land of the free and the home of the brave.

And where is the band who so vauntingly swore,
'Mid the havoc of war and the battle's confusion.
A home and a country they'd leave us no more?
Their blood has wash'd out their foul footstep's pollution.
No Refuge could save the hireling and slave
From the terror of flight or the gloom of the grave.
And the star-spangled banner in triumph doth wave
O'er the land of the free and the home of the brave.

O thus be it ever when free man shall stand,
Between their loved homes and the war's desolation.
Blest with vict'ry and peace, may the heav'n rescued land
Praise the Power that hath made and preserved us a nation!
And this be our motto, "In God is our trust!"
And the star-spangled banner in triumph shall wave
O'er the land of the free and the home of the brave.

You're A Grand Old Flag
Words and Music by George M. Cohan

George M. Cohan was a consummate showman. He wrote this rousing tribute to our flag in 1906 for a Broadway production titled *George Washington, Jr.* In this musical, he marched across the stage carrying the American flag while singing *You're A Grand Old Flag.* This image remains in the American consciousness as a symbol of patriotic fervor, and has become an icon of our American musical culture. In addition to this famous song, Cohan also wrote *I'm A Yankee Doodle Dandy,* and *Give My Regards To Broadway,* both Broadway classics, but his most famous song of all was composed during World War I and is titled, *Over There.* He died in New York City in 1942.

You're a grand old flag!
You're a high flying flag,
And forever in peace may you wave.
You're the emblem of the land I love,
The home of the free and the brave!
Ev'ry heart beats true
'Neath the Red, White and Blue
Where there's never a boast or brag.
But should auld acquaintance be forgot,
Keep your eye on the grand old flag.

Hal Leonard Student Piano Library

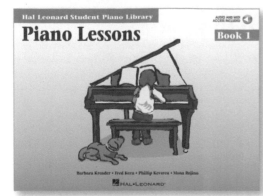

The Hal Leonard Student Piano Library has great music and solid pedagogy delivered in a truly creative and comprehensive method. It's that simple. A creative approach to learning using solid pedagogy and the best music produces skilled musicians! Great music means motivated students, inspired teachers and delighted parents. It's a method that encourages practice, progress, confidence, and best of all – success.

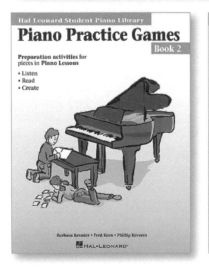

PIANO LESSONS BOOK 1
00296177 Book/Online Audio...........................$9.99
00296001 Book Only...$7.99

PIANO PRACTICE GAMES BOOK 1
00296002 ....$7.99

PIANO SOLOS BOOK 1
00296568 Book/Online Audio...........................$9.99
00296003 Book Only...$7.99

PIANO THEORY WORKBOOK BOOK 1
00296023 ....$7.50

PIANO TECHNIQUE BOOK 1
00296563 Book/Online Audio...........................$8.99
00296105 Book Only...$7.99

NOTESPELLER FOR PIANO BOOK 1
00296088 ....$7.99

TEACHER'S GUIDE BOOK 1
00296048 ....$7.99

PIANO LESSONS BOOK 2
00296178 Book/Online Audio...........................$9.99
00296006 Book Only...$7.99

PIANO PRACTICE GAMES BOOK 2
00296007 ....$8.99

PIANO SOLOS BOOK 2
00296569 Book/Online Audio...........................$8.99
00296008 Book Only...$7.99

PIANO THEORY WORKBOOK BOOK 2
00296024 ....$7.99

PIANO TECHNIQUE BOOK 2
00296564 Book/Online Audio...........................$8.99
00296106 Book Only...$7.99

NOTESPELLER FOR PIANO BOOK 2
00296089 ....$6.99

PIANO LESSONS BOOK 3
00296179 Book/Online Audio...........................$9.99
00296011 Book Only...$7.99

PIANO PRACTICE GAMES BOOK 3
00296012 ....$7.99

PIANO SOLOS BOOK 3
00296570 Book/Online Audio...........................$8.99
00296013 Book Only...$7.99

PIANO THEORY WORKBOOK BOOK 3
00296025 ....$7.99

PIANO TECHNIQUE BOOK 3
00296565 Book/Enhanced CD Pack..................$8.99
00296114 Book Only...$7.99

NOTESPELLER FOR PIANO BOOK 3
00296167 ....$7.99

PIANO LESSONS BOOK 4
00296180 Book/Online Audio...........................$9.99
00296026 Book Only...$7.99

PIANO PRACTICE GAMES BOOK 4
00296027 ....$6.99

PIANO SOLOS BOOK 4
00296571 Book/Online Audio...........................$8.99
00296028 Book Only...$7.99

PIANO THEORY WORKBOOK BOOK 4
00296038 ....$7.99

PIANO TECHNIQUE BOOK 4
00296566 Book/Online Audio...........................$8.99
00296115 Book Only...$7.99

PIANO LESSONS BOOK 5
00296181 Book/Online Audio...........................$9.99
00296041 Book Only...$8.99

PIANO SOLOS BOOK 5
00296572 Book/Online Audio...........................$9.99
00296043 Book Only...$7.99

PIANO THEORY WORKBOOK BOOK 5
00296042 ....$8.99

PIANO TECHNIQUE BOOK 5
00296567 Book/Online Audio...........................$8.99
00296116 Book Only...$8.99

ALL-IN-ONE PIANO LESSONS
00296761 Book A – Book/Online Audio $10.99
00296776 Book B – Book/Online Audio $10.99
00296851 Book C – Book/Online Audio $10.99
00296852 Book D – Book/Online Audio $10.99

Prices, contents, and availability subject to change without notice.

www.halleonard.com

0419
024